CONTENTS

Vendée

Lyon, page 10

WHAT'S HOT: FRANCE

Galeries Lafayette, Paris, p.12

France is one of the biggest countries in Europe. Whatever you're looking for, there is a good chance you will find it in France. These are just a few of the highlights you can find out more about later in the book.

1. THE PARIS CATACOMBS p.13

French Catacombs, p.13

France is full of historical sites, from Roman ruins to First World War memorials. But what could be spookier than a visit to the Paris Catacombs, where the walls are lined with the bones of the dead from centuries past?

2. SOCCA ON THE STREET p.18

Not the kind of street soccer that involves kicking a ball around. This is a famous street-food snack that is particularly popular in the southern city of Nice.

3. THE FRENCH GLASTONBURY p.24

France is a great place to hear live music of all kinds. Paris is especially good for a variety of bands and styles of music – but France's biggest music festival happens far to the west, in Brittany.

Vieilles Charrues, Brittany, p.24

4. RIDE THE AIGUILLE DU MIDI CABLE CAR p.28

France has two great mountain ranges, the Alps and the Pyrénées, which attract millions of hikers, bikers, skiers and snowboarders each year. Riding the cable-car from the mountain town of Chamonix to the peaks of the Aiguille du Midi is a great thrill.

THE REAL FRANCE

Your need-to-know guide for all things French

Anne-Marie Laval

First published in 2013
by Franklin Watts

Franklin Watts
338 Euston Road
London NW1 3BH

Franklin Watts Australia
Level 17/207 Kent Street
Sydney, NSW 2000

Series Editor: Sarah Peutrill
Series Designer: Sophie Wilkins
Picture researcher: Diana Morris

Dewey number: 914.4

HB ISBN: 978 1 4451 1968 7
Library ebook ISBN: 978 1 4451 2595 4

Printed in China

Franklin Watts is a division of Hachette Children's Books, an Hachette UK company.
www.hachette.co.uk

Picture credits:Adeliepenguin/Dreamstime: 16tl, 17c. Arras Festival: 20tc, 24t, Artens/Shutterstock: 18t, 42tr. Bocman1973/Shutterstock: 14-15. Youssouf Cader/ Dreamstime: 40t. John Cairs/Alamy: 10br. Enrico Carlone/Shutterstock: 1, 32tr. Caro/Alamy: 20b. Cata37/Dreamstime: 38tr. Corentin/Shutterstock: 8t. Tom Craig/Dreamstime: 36. Uli Danner/Dreamstime: 20tr, 21t. Defotoberg/Shutterstock: 5tc, 18b. Werner Dieterich/Alamy: 22. Sally Dillon/Getty Images: 33b. Directphoto/Dreamstime:7tl. Guylain Doyle/ Lonely Planet/Getty Images: 39t. Pierre-Jean Durieu/ Shutterstock: 11t. Emei/Shutterstock: 20tl, 20c. Extreme Sports Photo/Alamy: front cover t. Falk/ Shutterstock: 9b. Food & Drink Photos Superstock: 16bl. Simon C Ford/Alamy: 28t. Robert Fried/Alamy: 10t. Vlad G/Shutterstock: 2. Guillermo Pis Gonzalez/ Shutterstock: 6bl, 13t. Philippe Halle/Dreamstime: 40b. Louis Henault/Dreamstime: 5tl, 41b. Imagebroker/ Alamy: 28c. Jorisvo/Shutterstock: 26tc. Mike Finn-Kelcey/Alamy: 34b. Peter Kirillov/istockphoto: front cover bc, 9t. 35b.Leadinglights/Shutterstock: 11b. R J Lerich/Shutterstock: 38tc, 38c, 42tc. Lexan/ Shutterstock: 6c, 12b, 48-49, Lillisphotography/ istockphoto: 17t. Magspace/Shutterstock: front cover bl. M Meeds/Dreamstime: 37. Melba Photo Agency/ Alamy: 40c. Luciano Mortula/Shutterstock: 6tl. Laurence Mouton/Alamy: 30t. Neirfy/Shutterstock: 12t, 12c, 42tl. Marc Pagani Photography/Shutterstock: 26tl, 26c. Pecold/Shutterstock: 6tc, 32tl.. Petitgolo/Dreamstime: 19t. Daniele Pietrobelli/Shutterstock: 21b Plotniko/ Dreamstime: 42b. Plus99/Dreamstime: front cover br., 16tr. Paul Prescott/Shutterstock: 5cl. Frederic Prochasson/Shutterstock: 5br, 10bl, 47. Prometheus72/ Shutterstock: 5tr, 6tr, 26tr, 29t, 29c. Graue Razvan/ Shutterstock: 38tl, 38b. Radu Razvan /Shutterstock: 16tc, 27t, 43b. Realy Easy Star/Silvio Massolo/Alamy: 6br, 18c. Rock en Seine: 25t. David Rogers/Getty Images: 31. Rook76/Shutterstock: 41c. Andersen Ross/ Alamy: 32b. Kaushik Roy/Getty Images: 23. Edward Simons/Alamy: 19c. Kristy Sparrow/Getty Images: 30c. Steve Vidler/Alamy: 13b. Vieilles Charues: 6bc. Wikipedia: 35t.Stephan Zabel/istockphoto: 32tc, 34t. Zoonar/Rusian Olinchuck/Alamy: 27c.

Nice Carnival, p.36

5. WATCH A FOOTBALL MATCH
p.30

Every big city in France has a football team so there's plenty of choice. If there's a big international match on, you may be able to watch it on a giant outdoor screen for free.

6. PARTY AT THE NICE CARNIVAL p.36

Carnival celebrations happen across France, but Nice is thought to have held one of the first carnivals ever, anywhere. Since they have been practising for such a long time, the people of Nice know how to party properly!

7. EAT *FROMAGE DE TETE* IN CORSICA p.39

Actually, you might not want to: it means 'cheese of the head', and is made from pigs' brains. But you'll find plenty of things that ARE good to eat at a Corsican village festival.

IT'S (NEARLY) OFFICIAL!
TOP PLACES TO VISIT IN FRANCE

Members of one of the world's biggest travel websites picked these top French destinations:

1. Paris – the capital city could keep any visitor busy for a year or more!

2. Chamonix – Europe's mountain-sports capital.

3. Nice – down on the warm Mediterranean coast, Nice has a great vibe.

4. Cannes – home of film festivals and a great place for celebrity spotting.

5. Strasbourg – right by the border with Germany, this will show you a different side to France.

6. Biarritz – a beautiful city perched above the crashing waves of the Atlantic.

FRANCE FACTS AND STATS

Ancient volcano, Auvergne

France is the biggest country in Western Europe. Whether you're looking for relaxing hot beaches, the challenge of giant mountains, lively, noisy cities or quiet countryside, you'll find it somewhere here!

LANDSCAPE

France is mostly rolling countryside, but as you travel about you'll spot all kinds of other landscapes. Highlights to watch out for include:

- Worn-down old volcanoes in the Auvergne region
- Flat, wind-whipped lands stretching all the way to the horizon in the Vendée
- Water meadows in the north-east
- Giant, snow-capped mountains such as the Alps and Pyrénées.

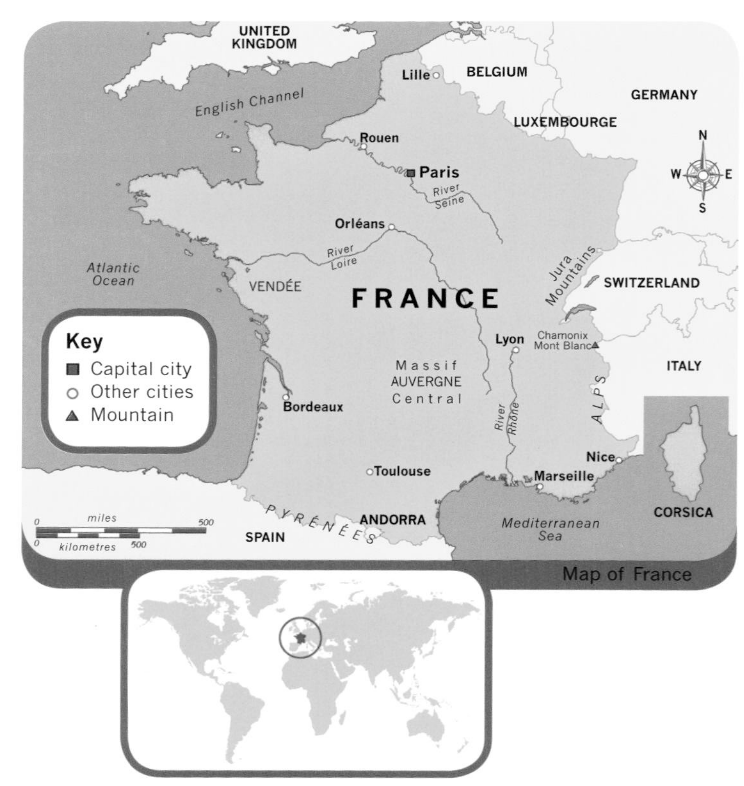

Map of France

CLIMATE

The weather in France changes throughout the year. On the far south coast it's nearly always warm and sunny, even in winter. In summer it can be incredibly hot.

The far north is different: winters can be cold and icy. If you're riding a bike along the famous cobbled roads of the north, watch out, it's easy to skid off! In summer, though, the north is warm enough for sunbathing and swimming in the sea. Parisians flee to the north-west coast in summer, to get away from the heat further south.

In the parts of France between these two extremes of north and south the weather is... well, in between!

North coast, summertime

Alsace in the north-east

FACT FILE ONE

CAPITAL CITY: Paris

AREA: 551,500 km² (European territory), 643,801 km² (including overseas territory)

HIGHEST POINT: Mont Blanc (4,807 m)

LOWEST POINT: delta of the River Rhone (2 m below sea level)

LONGEST RIVER: Loire (1,012 km)

BORDERS: mainland France has borders with, from north to south, Luxembourg, Belgium, Germany, Switzerland, Italy, Monaco, Spain and Andorra

NATURAL HAZARDS: floods, avalanches, droughts, high winds and forest fires

PEOPLE

Pelota, traditional Basque game

In France, people's attachment to their region is very strong. In the Basque country, for example, people might tell you they are Basque rather than French. Brittany, Corsica, Provence and Savoy also have strong regional identities, with their own cooking, music, stories, games and sometimes their own language.

Some French people's families originally came from other countries, particularly those in North Africa. Although these people are French, they also have their own separate culture.

Apartment living in Lyon

URBAN LIFE

Most French people live in cities. Living spaces are often quite cramped: many people live in small apartments, not houses, with only a small balcony for outside space. But the advantage of living in a city is that you're close to school, work, clubs, music venues, cafés and sports clubs. If they can afford it, people often own a place in the countryside, where they can escape from the busy city life.

RURAL LIFE

Life in rural France is very different from the cities. Many people work on the land. The small villages or hamlets might have only five or ten houses. Tiny two-seater diesel cars are a common sight. They don't go very fast, so it can take people a long time to get to the shops!

Lyon's city centre

FACT FILE TWO

POPULATION: 62 million (European territory), 65 million (including overseas territory)

CITY POPULATION: Paris (10.41 million), Marseille (1.457 million), Lyon (1.456 million), Lille (1.028 million)

AGE STRUCTURE: 18.7% under 15 years old; 63.8% 15–64 years old; 17.5% over 64 years old

YOUTH UNEMPLOYMENT (15–24 year-olds): 22.6%

OBESITY: 16.9%

LANGUAGES: French (official language), German, Italian, Arabic. Regional languages include Basque, Provencal, Breton, Alsatian, Corsican, Catalan and Flemish.

RELIGIONS: Roman Catholic (85%), Muslim (5–10%), Protestant (2%), Jewish (1%)

Traditional houses, French Pyrenees

PARIS

France's capital city, Paris, is huge. Well over 10 million people live in the urban area, called 'metropolitan Paris'. At the heart of the metro area lies the ancient City of Paris – the place most visitors head straight for.

A FREE LOOKOUT

One of the best places for a view of Paris is the Eiffel Tower. The trouble is, it's expensive and busy! **Instead, try:**

1. SACRE COEUR

The view from the steps to this beautiful white church, which is on a hill in the Montmartre district, is breathtaking. You'll DEFINITELY be out of breath if you decide to climb the 234 steps that spiral to the top of the church dome.

2. ARC DE TRIOMPHE

At 6.30 every evening, a ceremony is held to remember those who died fighting for France. Afterwards, climb the 280 steps to the top of the Arc for an amazing view of the busy Champs Elysées, Paris's best-known street.

3. GALERIES LAFAYETTE

The most famous department store in Paris is worth a visit for its beautiful interior. After you've had a wander around, climb up to the roof terrace for the view of the Palais Garnier, Montmartre, the Eiffel Tower and the Arc de Triomphe.

Galeries Lafayette, Paris

THE CATACOMBS

Ready for a spooky visit? Then head for the Paris Catacombs! You follow a winding stairway, then an underground passage to a doorway. Above it are the words "**Stop! This is the Empire of Death!**" Step through, and you see that the walls of this underground maze are lined with skulls and other bones. They are the remains of dead Parisians, stored here since the late 1700s.

"When Paris sneezes, Europe catches cold."
—German Prime Minister Metternich describes Paris's importance in the 1800s.

AN IMMIGRANT CITY

Immigrants have been coming to Paris for centuries. Two in every five Parisians have at least one parent who's an immigrant, and 37% of all new immigrants to France live in the city.

Today, most immigrants come from Africa or Asia. So if you want to hear North African music, eat Vietnamese food, or visit a display of art from Mali, Paris is a great place to do it!

PARIS
A WALKING TOUR

There are lots of professional walking tours of Paris, led by guides. But they're quite expensive, and they mostly visit places older people are interested in. Why not try our movies-and-gore-based walking tour of Paris instead?

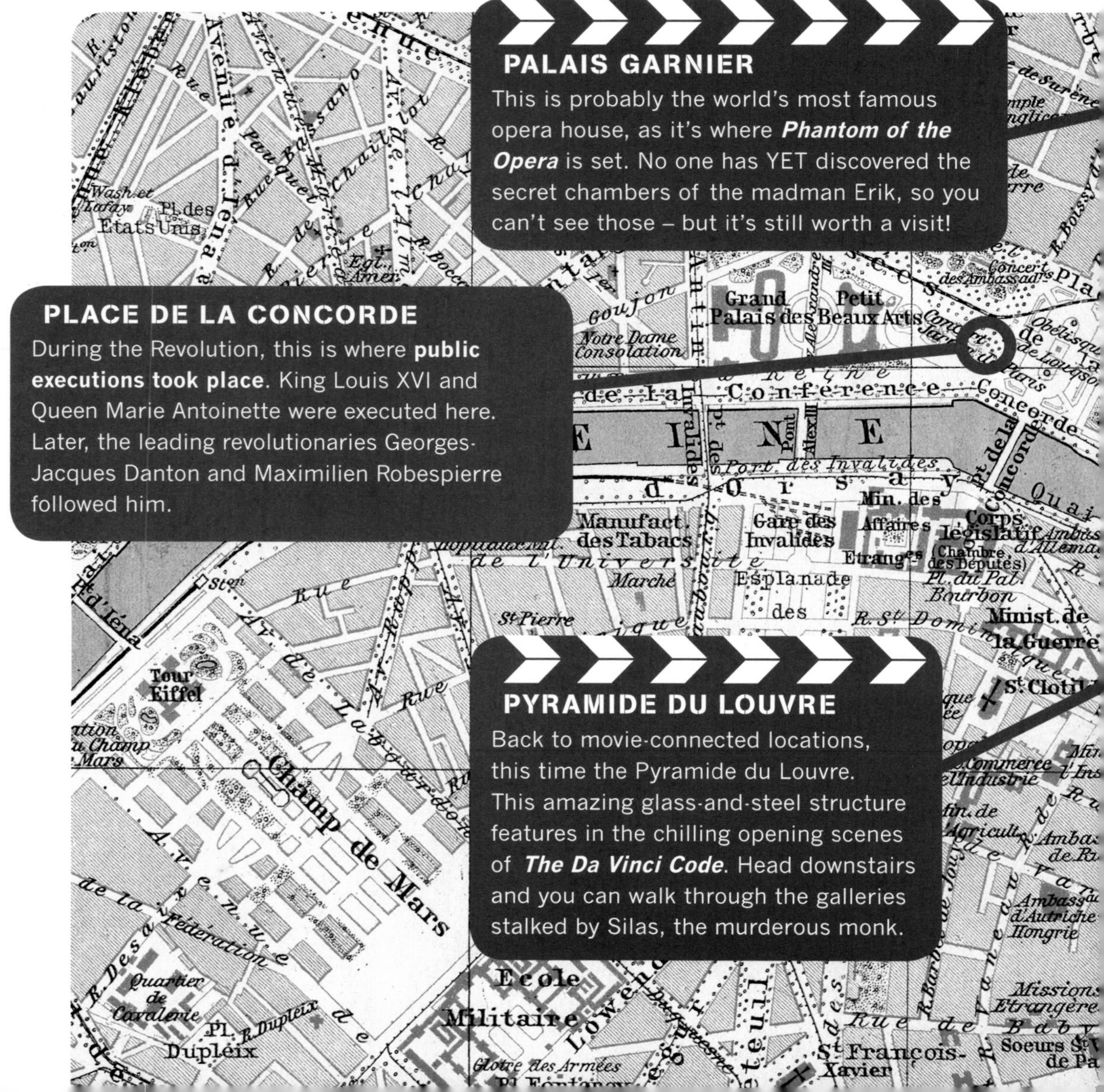

PALAIS GARNIER

This is probably the world's most famous opera house, as it's where ***Phantom of the Opera*** is set. No one has YET discovered the secret chambers of the madman Erik, so you can't see those – but it's still worth a visit!

PLACE DE LA CONCORDE

During the Revolution, this is where **public executions took place**. King Louis XVI and Queen Marie Antoinette were executed here. Later, the leading revolutionaries Georges-Jacques Danton and Maximilien Robespierre followed him.

PYRAMIDE DU LOUVRE

Back to movie-connected locations, this time the Pyramide du Louvre. This amazing glass-and-steel structure features in the chilling opening scenes of ***The Da Vinci Code***. Head downstairs and you can walk through the galleries stalked by Silas, the murderous monk.

PARIS AT THE MOVIES

Want to check out a movie featuring Paris before you visit? Try these:

The Bourne Identity, **starring Matt Damon, has great shots of Paris beside the River Seine, and a top-notch car chase through the city.**

Funny Face**, starring Audrey Hepburn, about a New York shop assistant whisked away to Paris for a photo shoot by a fashion photographer, after being spotted in the background of one of his photos.**

PONT NEUF

If you've seen ***The Bourne Identity*** (see panel), you've already seen the Pont Neuf. Its name means 'New Bridge', but this is actually the oldest bridge across the river! It's a great place to watch the river traffic.

NOTRE DAME DE PARIS CATHEDRAL

Notre Dame is famous as a beautiful Gothic building. We're here, though, because this is the setting for ***The Hunchback of Notre Dame***, the tragic love story featuring the hunchback Quasimodo and the beautiful gypsy Esmeralda.

CONCIERGERIE

What good is a walking tour without a bit of gore? During the French Revolution, the Conciergerie was a **terrifying prison**. It was also the last known address of Queen Marie Antoinette, and at least **2,500** others, before they were executed.

A COUNTRY BUILT ON LUNCH

One of the things that might take you by surprise about France is the way almost *everything* stops for lunch. If you can't afford to go into a restaurant, it's easy to be stranded without anything to eat. Outside the cities, every bakery and corner shop will be closed for hours!

Picnic lunch, French style

THE 12.30 RUSH HOUR

At 12.30pm, most towns and villages have a mini rush hour. It happens when everyone heads home for lunch. No one really wants to sit down and eat after 1pm – it's seen as a bit uncivilised. People who cannot get home don't miss out. French roads are littered with picnic places, so they can pull over and stop for lunch (left). Or restaurants offer a *menu du jour*, meal of the day.

"It costs a few euros more than a sandwich and a drink, but then [people] don't start snacking at five o'clock because a sandwich hasn't really satisfied them."

— restaurant owner Otis Lebert explains why a proper lunch is such a good idea.

THE MAIN MEAL

Lunch is traditionally the main meal in France. There are two or three courses: in a restaurant, the menu du jour usually includes a starter such as soup, a meat or fish dish with vegetables and a dessert or cheese.

This kind of lunch takes over an hour, and often more than two. Afterwards people have a little rest before going back to work. This still happens in the countryside and small towns, but in the cities things are changing. People eat less, finish quickly and head back to work.

Pavement café, Arles, Provence

> **"I thought, let's just get there. THEN we'll have lunch!"**
>
> — Greg Lemond, the only American winner of the Tour de France bike race (see pp. 26–27), on the French habit of stopping for a two-hour lunch break in the middle of a long journey.

EATING IN THE EVENING

In the evening, at about 8pm, French people traditionally ate a smaller meal. Often it was leftovers from lunch, bulked up with bread or pasta. Today, though, larger evening meals are becoming more common. Maybe that's why 16.9% of French people are now dangerously overweight.

FOOD

STREET FOOD

Breakfast croissants

Sandwiches, croissants and other bread-based street foods are available all over France.

Just look for a sign saying *Boulangerie*, which is French for bakery. Around France you'll also find all sorts of local fast-food dishes you can eat sitting on a bench or a beach.

THE SOUTH

The cities of southern France are heaven for street food. Nice is especially good. Socca is one of the local delicacies. It's a savoury chickpea pancake, traditionally cooked using a blazing-hot wooden oven. Ask for a portion, and the chef pours chickpea batter into a sizzling-hot copper pan, with a thick layer of olive oil in the bottom. When it's cooked he scrapes the pancake into paper. Once you've tasted the combination of crispy base and chewy top layer, you'll never want another burger!

Giant pan of socca, southern France

Spicy merguez sausages – kebab in a skin!

East of Nice, many people speak Italian as well as French. The food is Italian-influenced too: the pizza stalls on the side of the road are as good as pizzerias in Italy itself. West of Nice, around Marseille, there are many immigrants from North Africa. This is a great area to find street food such as falafel, grilled corn on the cob and spicy merguez sausages.

In the Alps, traditional foods feature things that would keep through the long Alpine winter: cheese, potatoes and dried meat. *Tartiflette* is a kind of open pie featuring all three, and is a great dish to try to see if you like the region's food.

Cooking a gigantic tartiflette

FAST FOOD IN THE NORTH

Regional fast-food specialities from northern France:

NORTH AND NORTHWEST

This is the land of the *galette*, a thick pancake that's eaten piping hot, folded around egg, cheese and ham. It may also be easten wtih fish, vegetables, apple slices or berries.

NORTHEAST

Close to the border with Belgium (where chips were invented!) you'll find stalls selling chips and sausage. Nearer to Germany you might also be offered *choucroute* – pickled cabbage. You don't have to accept!

MUSIC

Wherever you go in France, you'll hear music being played on car stereos, in cafés and restaurants, live on street corners, and in concert venues. So, what kind of music can you expect to hear?

Amateur musicians in Paris

A diner gets carried away as she sings a chanson

CHANSON

Chanson is actually just French for 'song', but this is a particular kind of song. It's one that tells a story, and the words often jumble strangely against the tune, in a way that sounds odd unless you're used to it. If that sounds a bit uninspiring, try thinking of it as rap for elderly French people!

REGIONAL MUSIC

Many French regions have their own traditional music, including:

Mediterranean coast
Gypsy and flamenco-influenced music

Corsica
Eerie, polyphonic singing

Alps and Pyrénées
Combinations of pipe and drum music

Auvergne and Vendée
Bagpipe music; also the hurdy gurdy (a bizarre mechanical violin)

Flamenco guitar player, Avignon

The hurdy gurdy

MODERN MUSIC

Fortunately for younger visitors, there's plenty of modern music in France. Rock, heavy metal, pop and house music are all popular. Each sounds very like the same type of music in other countries. In fact, sometimes the songs ARE the same. You'll find yourself thinking a tune sounds familiar – then realise it's a song you already know, but sung in French.

LIVE MUSIC

LIVE MUSIC VENUES

Live music of all sorts is played in small venues around France. One of the best places to see music is Paris. Top venues include:

L'Alimentation Genérale,
for Latin American, jazz, hip-hop and funk

Le Batofar,
a concert venue on a boat in the River Seine, with all kinds of different bands

Au Café de Paris,
upstairs – bands, poetry, and theatre; downstairs in the cellar – young rock and punk bands

Le Klub
bands pumping out raucous French rock or Goth heavy metal

Outdoor rappers

RAI AND RAP

Rai is a kind of music brought to France by immigrants from Algeria. At one time France governed Algeria, and many immigrants still come to France from there. Rai is most popular among France's North African communities. The lyrics sometimes use a French-Arab secret language called *verlan* (see box).

Hip-hop and rap are also popular among immigrants, as well as other young French people. Stars such as MC Solaar were among the first French rappers. Today, listen out for Oxmo Pucchino, Lunatik or ATC.

ZOUK

Zouk comes from the French Caribbean islands of Guadeloupe and Martinique. The music is a combination of Caribbean and Latin American dance music. The word zouk means 'party', and zouk is music for dancing to. In fact, you should be able to find a zouk dance class in Paris or other large cities. You can also listen to zouk-style music on French radio.

Zouk dance performance

VERLAN

Verlan is a secret language among immigrants from North Africa. It's not as secret as it used to be, though! Today, some verlan words have made it into everyday French slang.

Verlan works by changing around the front and back of words. The best way to explain this is the word verlan itself:

1. The French word for 'inverse', meaning changed round, is *l'invers*. This is pronounced *lan-ver*.

2. Swap the front and back around, and you get *verlan*.

Other common *verlan* words include:

Jourbon (from *bonjour*, hello)

Meuf (from *femme*, woman)

Beur (from *arabe*, Arab)

Bléca (from *cablé*, wired; in verlan it means cool, trendy)

Céfran (from *français*, French)

Ouf (from *fou*, crazy)

FESTIVALS AND LIVE MUSIC

Music festivals similar to Reading or the V Festival are popular in France. In fact, live music is generally easy to find. Almost every celebration, from tiny village fêtes high in the Alps to huge city carnivals, will have a live band or two.

Coldplay perform at Main Square festival, Arras

THE FRENCH GLASTONBURY

Fancy a visit to the French equivalent to Glastonbury? Then you need to head for Brittany (and not because it rains more in Brittany than elsewhere in France.*) It's because Brittany is home to the Vieilles Charrues music festival, the biggest in Vieilles Charrues takes place on the outskirts of the city of Carhaix. It lasts four days, and over a quarter of a million people turn up. The music is a combination of big international acts and almost unknown local bands. The festival is famous for its relaxed, friendly atmosphere.

*Though it does, but still nowhere NEAR as much as at Glastonbury.

MUSIC FESTIVAL YEAR

You could easily spend a summer travelling around France from festival to festival:

APRIL

Printemps de Bourges (Bourges, central France)

Rock, pop, folk, world, hip-hop and R&B mean there is something for nearly everyone here.

MAY

Nuits Sonores (Lyon, southern France)

Mainly dance and electronica, but with a healthy dose of rock and pop thrown in.

Rock en Seine

JUNE

Main Square Festival (Arras, northern France)

Mostly rock and pop music, but with quite a lot of dance and electronica as well.

JULY

Sonisphere (Amnéville, northeastern France)

One for the metalheads! This is three days of mostly heavy metal and rock music.

AUGUST

Rock en Seine (Paris)

Finish your festival summer with a trip to Paris for a final helping of rock and pop. Trivia fact: this is the festival where Oasis split up in 2009.

Vieilles Charrues

CYCLING AND THE TOUR DE FRANCE

If you started your visit to France in Paris, you'll have seen bikes from the *Vélib* bike-hire scheme everywhere. These are a popular, easy way to whiz around the city. Parisians aren't alone in their love of bicycles: the whole country is mad about cycling!

THE TOUR DE FRANCE

Nothing shows how French people love cycling more than the Tour de France bike race. Each year, millions of people line the roads to watch the riders whiz past.

The Tour finishes on the Champs Élysées in Paris. Before that, the riders have spent most of July racing through the rest of France. The route travels in a giant circle around the country: in French it is sometimes called *La Grande Boucle*, or The Giant Loop. The route changes each year, and goes clockwise one year, anti-clockwise the next.

Mass sprint, Tour de France

"Whenever I see an adult on a bicycle, I have hope for the future of the human race."

— Science fiction writer H.G. Wells

RACING IN THE MOUNTAINS

The Tour always visits the Alps and Pyrénées. The riders sometimes have to ride uphill for 100 km or more – often three or four days in a row. These mountain stages are great to watch, because the racers are going slower and it is possible to see more of the action.

Solo mountain breakaway, Tour de France

BRILLIANT BIKE RACES

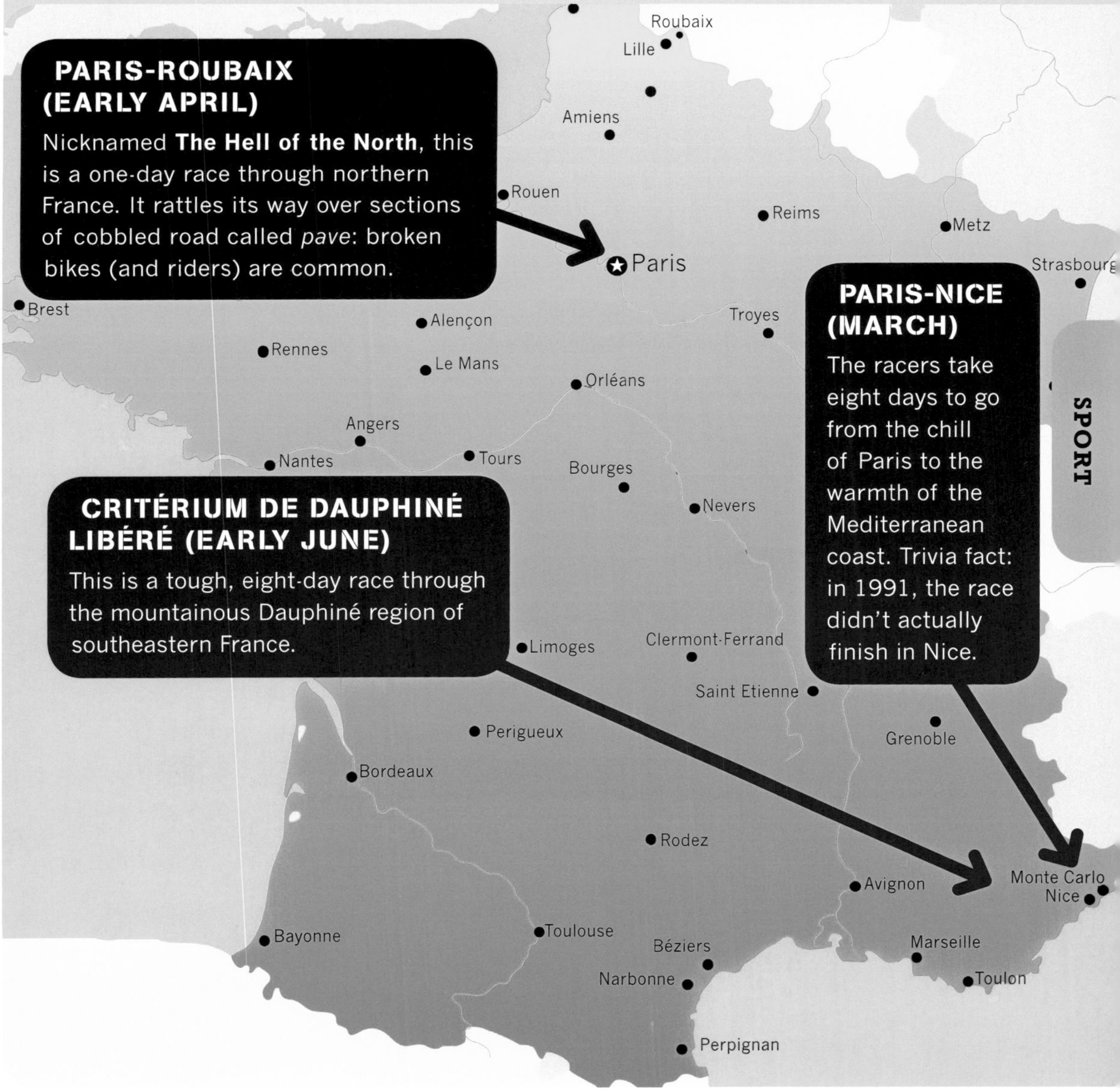

PARIS-ROUBAIX (EARLY APRIL)

Nicknamed **The Hell of the North**, this is a one-day race through northern France. It rattles its way over sections of cobbled road called *pave*: broken bikes (and riders) are common.

PARIS-NICE (MARCH)

The racers take eight days to go from the chill of Paris to the warmth of the Mediterranean coast. Trivia fact: in 1991, the race didn't actually finish in Nice.

CRITÉRIUM DE DAUPHINÉ LIBÉRÉ (EARLY JUNE)

This is a tough, eight-day race through the mountainous Dauphiné region of southeastern France.

FUN IN THE MOUNTAINS

France has territory in the Alps and the Pyrénées, and both are popular with visitors. If there's one place that is guaranteed to give you a taste of the mountain lifestyle, it's the Alpine town of Chamonix. And no wonder – Chamonix lies next door to Mont Blanc, the highest mountain in Western Europe.

Urban biker, Chamonix

FIVE THINGS TO DO IN CHAMONIX BEFORE YOU LEAVE

1. RIDE THE AIGUILLE DU MIDI CABLE CAR

The peak of the Aiguille du Midi

It's so high that many people feel a bit dizzy when they get off. Those bright-coloured spots you see out on the snowfields are the tents of mountaineers climbing Mont Blanc.

2. SWIM IN THE PUBLIC POOL

Chamonix's outdoor, Olympic-sized swimming pool is a real treat. Where else can you do backstroke while enjoying a view of Mont Blanc's snowy summit?

3. HYDRO-GLISSE THROUGH TOWN

Hydro-glisse is a bit like whitewater rafting on a bodyboard. Try it on the River Arve, which flows right through the middle of town.

4. VISIT THE SEA OF ICE

The Montenvers train will take you to the *Mer de Glace* (Sea of Ice) glacier. Though global warming is causing it to shrink, the glacier is still an amazing sight.

5. TRY THE LUGE D'ÉTÉ

Luge d'Été means 'summer luge'. You slide down the mountainside, steering a rickety old go-kart down a snaking cement half-pipe.

"I came to Chamonix for a gap year, but I'm 43 now. It's turned into a gap life!"

— Andy, Chamonix downhill mountain biker

FIRST TO THE TOP

At the centre of Chamonix is a statue of Jacques Balmat (far left), a local mountain guide who, in 1786, was the first to climb Mont Blanc. Beside him is Horace-Bénédict de Saussure, who is often called the founder of mountaineering.

Climbers below the Mont Blanc summit

OTHER MOUNTAIN TOWNS TO VISIT

ANNECY

Beside a beautiful lake in the French Alps, Annecy is one of the prettiest towns in France. You can try practically any sport, from rock climbing to scuba diving.

MORZINE/ LES-GETS

These two villages in the Alps are now a world-famous mountain-biking destination in summer, and a ski/ snowboard resort in the winter.

BAGNÉRES DE LUCHON

Luchon, at the foot of the Pyrénées, is a smart resort town, but is also popular with extreme sportspeople. It's not uncommon to see muddy mountain bikers cruising past the swanky shops.

FOOTBALL AND RUGBY

Tennis is everywhere

Traditional sports are just as popular in France as newer ones such as surfing or skateboarding. Tennis, basketball, and motorbike and car races always draw big crowds. France's favourite sports, though, are probably football and rugby.

FOOTBALL

Football is the most popular spectator sport in France. During the season (which runs from August until May), the parks are full of kids playing in local leagues. The young players are probably dreaming of one day copying their heroes, players such as Zlatan Ibrahimovic, who plays for Paris-St-Germain, or Yoann Gourcuff of Olympique Lyonnais.

France supporters watch a match on a giant public screen

TOP TEAMS TO WATCH

Ligue 1 is the top football league in France. Every big city has a football team, so wherever you are, you will be able to watch a match.

Northwest: Brest, Lorient, Rennes

Northeast: Lille, Paris-St-Germain, Valenciennes

Southwest: Bordeaux, Toulouse

Southeast: Marseilles, Montpellier, Nice

> **"I eat football, I sleep football, I breathe football."**
>
> — Thierry Henry, one of the best-ever French footballers.

RUGBY

Rugby is especially popular in the south of France. The top league is called the 'Top 14' (in French, the top *quatorze*). The best seats are expensive, but at many clubs you can go and buy a match ticket for just a few euros, if you don't mind standing at pitch-level. It makes it hard to follow the action, but the atmosphere is great!

TOULON RUGBY

The Top 14 rugby club Toulon's president, Mourad Boudjellal, is a rugby-mad comic book millionaire. He has spent a fortune filling Toulon's team sheet with international superstars. Today, the team is like a rugby version of Real Madrid football club and its *galácticos*.

Fanatical fans of Toulon, French rugby super team

LE WEEKEND

Most French people live in cities. *Le weekend* is a chance for them to get away from the busy city life and enjoy a different part of France. As a result, every Friday night across the country, lots of people pack up their cars and head off for a short break.

BORROWED WORDS

Le weekend isn't the only English word to have crept into the French language. Here are a few more:

- *le fun*
- *le hamburger*
- *le fast food*
- *le blog*

SUNDAYS IN FRANCE

French people think of Sunday in particular as a day of rest – or at least, a day when people should not really have to go to work. Many shops are closed all day. On Sunday mornings, local clubs meet up early, for cycling, hunting, hiking or other activities. People like to make sure they are home in time for lunch, when the whole family gets together. Being invited to Sunday lunch with a French family is a great honour!

Outside French family dining

TOP BREAKS FOR LE WEEKEND

There are endless possibilities for French weekend breaks – here are just three:

NORTH: ÉTRETAT

One of many resorts on the north coast, Étretat has a great market, a lovely beach and famous rock arches to the west of town. There is also a good campsite within walking distance of the centre.

CENTRAL FRANCE: PUY DE DÔME

Puy de Dôme is an extinct volcano. During summer there are all kinds of things to do here, from cycling and hiking to visiting Roman ruins. The area is famous for paragliding – thrill seekers can hitch a ride on a tandem!

SOUTH: WALKING AROUND CAP FERRAT

Cap Ferrat is one of the most expensive places in the most expensive part of France: the Côte d'Azur. A public footpath goes right around the Cap, and from it you can gawk at the enormous villas of Europe's billionaires.

Cycle touring in the Alps

ACCOMMODATION

There are all kinds of weekend accommodation available. Many families have holiday homes or apartments, inherited from a distant relative and now shared between the whole family. Other people stay in hotels or guest houses, or rent an apartment for a couple of days. Camping is also very popular (see pages 34–35).

CAMPING

There are all kinds of accommodation in France, from luxurious hotels to stone huts in the mountains. Probably the most popular of all – in summer, at least – is camping. Big white campervans are a common sight, but lots of people prefer camping in a tent.

Typical French campsite

A CAMPING DAY

09:00

Wake up in your tent to a tooting noise. It's the bread van! Join the queue of people waiting to buy fresh bread for breakfast.

10:00

Get on your bicycle and pedal off on one of the local cycle routes. These connect many coastal towns.

12:30

Back at the campsite for lunch: more bread, cheese and a salad. After that, it's time for a little snooze.

15:00

Head for the beach: it's low tide, a good time for digging in the sand and collecting shellfish.

17:00

Return to the campsite to clean the shellfish, before eating them with bread and salad. By 21:00 it is getting dark, and most people head for bed!

Hunting for shellfish, Noirmoutier (see p.35)

THE PASSAGE DU GOIS

Noirmoutier is an island off the west coast of France. The Passage du Gois is a causeway linking the island to the mainland. The sea covers it at high tide. As the water rises, crowds gather, to see if a driver will leave it too late and get caught by the ocean!

CAMPING HOTSPOTS

There are camping grounds all over France, but some areas are especially popular:

THE ALPS

Top pick:
The valley of the Verdon River – very beautiful, and good for whitewater rafting and rock climbing – is lined with campsites.

WEST COAST

Top pick:
The Quiberon Peninsula is great for watersports of all kinds, and close to the famous ancient standing stones of Carnac.

MEDITERRANEAN COAST

Top pick:
For the full-on Mediterranean experience, you can't beat the campsites on the coast near St Tropez.

Most campsites are less precarious than this one!

FESTIVALS

Nice Carnival – possibly the original carnival

If you stumble across a local festival during a trip to France, you've hit the jackpot. People bring food, there are local drinks, music, and a real party atmosphere. Of course, French festivals aren't limited to small local affairs. There are plenty of big ones that are worth a visit...

CARNIVAL:

Last Tuesday before Lent

Nice is thought to be where the first carnivals anywhere happened, in the 1200s. Today, over a million people flock to the city to enjoy two weeks of parades and parties. The 'flower battles', where crowds are bombarded with flowers, are great fun.

VICTORY DAY:

8 May

Victory Day celebrates the defeat of the German forces that invaded France during the Second World War (1939–45). You see French flags everywhere, and people like to sing patriotic songs. Generally this is a happy day, though everyone remembers those who died in the fighting.

BASTILLE DAY:

14 July

On 14 July 1789, angry citizens captured the notorious Bastille prison in Paris. It was a key event in the French Revolution, and today Bastille Day is France's biggest festival. There are street parties and processions across the country, and in Paris there is a huge parade.

> **"It is the great image of national unity... for which we would all stand, willing to die if necessary."**
>
> — Henri Martin, chairman of the French Senate in 1880, talks about Bastille Day.

Bastille Day, Paris

LA TOUSSAINT: **1 November**

In English this is called All Saints' Day. In France, La Toussaint is a quiet day when people remember the dead. Shops and other businesses close, and families go to visit the graves of family members and friends, or relatives who live far away.

NATIONAL HOLIDAYS

DATE:	HOLIDAY:
1 January	New Year's Day/*Premier de l'an*
Changeable	Good Friday/*Vendredi Saint*
Changeable	Easter Monday/*Lundi de Pâques*
1 May	May Day/*Fête du Travail*
8 May	Victory Day/*Victoire 1945*
Changeable	Ascension Day/*Ascension*
Changeable	Whit Monday/*Lundi de Pentecote*
14 July	Bastille Day/*Fête National*
15 August	Feast of the Assumption/*Assomption*
1 November	All Saints Day/*la Toussaint*
11 November	Armistice Day/*Armistice 1918*
25 December	Christmas Day/*Noël*
26 December	St Stephen's Day/*St Étienne*

CORSICA

Corsica is a large island off the south coast of France. Until the mid 1700s, it was part of Italy. The blend of French, Italian, and Corsican culture, the island's dramatic scenery and the beautiful beaches have made this a hot spot for visitors.

Traditional Corsican town houses

Blue seas and warm weather draw visitors

MOUNTAINS AND BEACHES

Corsica was formed by tremendous volcanic eruptions, which created the steep-sided mountains that make up most of the land. The tallest peak is Monte Cinto, which at 2,706 metres is over twice as high as Ben Nevis. There are 20 other mountains over 2,000 metres high: Corsica is very popular with hikers and climbers!

Lots of people also visit Corsica for the beaches. The island has over 1,000 km of coastline, and there are more than 200 beaches to choose from.

CORSICAN CULTURE

Almost every weekend, there is a festival of local art, music, cooking, or all three. Most villages and towns have a festival at least once a year, and these can be a great place to try the local food. Wild boar stew, crayfish, oysters and *brocciu* cheese are all local delicacies. Watch out for *fromage de tete*, though – it's 'head cheese', made from pigs' brains!

Corsican singers in action

ANCIENT HISTORY OF CORSICA

566 BCE
Ancient Greeks found the city of Aléria.

237 BCE
Romans take control of Corsica and make Aléria the capital city.

400s CE
Fall of Rome.

400s to 1347
Corsica falls victim to raiders from across the Mediterranean, including North Africa.

1347
Italian city-state of Genoa takes control of the island.

1769
Corsica conquered by France.

FAMOUS CORSICANS

The most famous Corsican is Napoleon Bonaparte, born in 1769 in Ajaccio. He was the Emperor of France from 1804 to 1815.

The northern town of Calvi claims that Christopher Columbus (who sailed to North America in 1492) was born there.

CORSICA FACT FILE

AREA: 8,680 km^2

POPULATION: 302,000 (2008)

COMMUNICATIONS: Ferries connect Corsica to southern France, the west coast of Italy, and the Italian island of Sardinia to the south

PHYSICAL FEATURES: Mountains run from north to south, and cover about 65% of the island

LANGUAGE: the official language is French; about 50% of people also speak Corsu, which is similar to Italian

OVERSEAS TERRITORIES

Réunion (see page 41)

France has territories around the world. Many are considered part of France, and send deputies to the national parliament. These overseas territories are very different from France, but are still influenced by French culture.

FRENCH POLYNESIA

French Polynesia is a large group of islands in the Pacific Ocean. The main island is Tahiti, which is where flights from mainland France arrive. July is a great time to visit: the Heiva festival celebrates not only the storming of the Bastille, but also Tahitian culture. Watch for the lines of *otea* dancers (otea is similar to Hawaiian hula dancing), and try *ia ota*, raw tuna in coconut milk and lime juice.

French colonial house, French Polynesia

French flags, Caribbean town hall

CARIBBEAN TERRITORIES

In the Caribbean, French territory includes the islands of Guadeloupe and Martinique, and French Guiana on the South American mainland. The two islands are popular tourist spots, famous for their snorkelling, diving and nightlife.

GUADELOUPE AND SPORT

Guadeloupe has produced an amazing number of top sportspeople, including footballers Lilian Thuram and Louis Saha; athletes Marie-José Perec and Christine Arron; and rugby star Mattheu Bastareaud.

THE INDIAN OCEAN

In the Indian Ocean, the islands of Mayotte and Réunion* are both French. Réunion, like Hawaii in the Pacific Ocean, is located above a volcanic 'hot spot'. The Piton de la Fournaise volcano is still active, and is constantly monitored for signs of an eruption.

***Random trivia fact:** Réunion is the part of the European Union furthest from Europe.

ST PIERRE AND MIQUELON

St Pierre and Miquelon are possibly France's most surprising territories. They are tiny islands off the coast of Canada. These 241 km^2 are a remnant from the 1700s, when France claimed to own about 25% of North America.

Harbour and lighthouse, St Pierre and Miquelon

KEY INFORMATION FOR TRAVELLERS

LANGUAGE

English is spoken in many tourist areas. Even so, trying to speak a few words of French (see page 44) before you switch to English usually gets a better reaction.

ENTERING FRANCE

People from European Union countries can enter France without a visa, though visitors arriving at airports and ferry ports usually have to show their passport.

Visitors from other countries may need a visa, so it is important to check with your own government whether this is required.

GETTING AROUND

France has a good railway system connecting its cities and towns. The train company is called SNCF. Buses are available in large cities and towns, though in rural areas they can be infrequent. Cycling is generally a good way to get around, though it is not always possible to take your bike on a train during a longer trip.

Container port, Le Havre

HEALTH

Pharmacies, which you can spot by the green cross outside, are a good source of help with minor health problems. Some pharmacy trivia: a sign showing a snake wound around a dagger means the pharmacist can tell you whether mushrooms you have gathered are safe to eat.

If you need to see a doctor in France, you will see either one registered with the Department of Health or one from a private practice. The Department of Health doctors have their fees set by the government, but private doctors are more expensive.

POSTAL SERVICES

Post boxes are coloured yellow, and there are plenty available. You can buy stamps at post offices (*La Poste*) or at any tobacconist's shop (*Tabac*). Post within France takes 2–3 days; post going abroad usually takes about a week.

MOBILE NETWORKS

The main European mobile phone networks are available in France. Orange is the biggest supplier. Using a foreign phone – even on the same network – is expensive, especially for data, so it's important to turn off data roaming.

INTERNET PROVISION

France lags behind other European countries in Internet service, particularly wifi, though it is slowly catching up. Wifi zones are available in cafés and at some town halls (called *mairie* in French), but you almost always have to get a pass code and log in to use them, and it is rarely free.

French café culture

CURRENCY:

Euro (€1 = roughly £0.80, or $1.30). Currency exchange at some banks, bureaux de change, large supermarkets and train stations.

TELEPHONE DIALLING CODES:

To call France from outside, dial your country's exit code plus 33, and drop the zero.

To call another country from France, add 00 and the country code of the place you are dialling to the beginning of the number, and drop the zero.

TIME ZONE:

Central European Time (CET): Greenwich Mean Time (GMT) +1 hour
In March, France switches to daylight-saving time, and clocks are put forward one hour. In October they are returned to CET.

OPENING HOURS:

Opening hours tend to be different in the city from the countryside, and in different parts of France. As a rough guide, most shops open between 09:00 and 10:00, close for at least an hour (but usually longer) some time between 12:30 and 14:30, and shut for the day at 19:00 or 20:00.

USEFUL PHRASES:

Bonjour/Au revoir	Hello/Goodbye
Parlez-vous anglais?	Do you speak English?
Désolé, je n'ai pas compris	Sorry, I didn't understand.
Merci/Non merci	Thank you/No, thank you
Pouvez-vous m'aider?	Can you help me?
Où se trouve...?	Where is... ?
Quel est le prix?	How much does it cost?

FINDING OUT MORE

BOOKS TO READ: NON-FICTION

Young Reporter in France: *Series* (Franklin Watts, 2011)
In this series, Ryan the Young Reporter finds out all about how French young people live including their home life, schooling, how they have fun and celebrate special days. The books include some key French phrases and test your knowledge of France with the mini quizzes.

Horrible Histories: *France* Terry Deary and Martin Brown (Scholastic, 2011)
Gruesome and otherwise astounding facts from French history, presented in the classic Horrible Histories style.

Bonjour France! Rebecca Welby (illustrator) (Beautiful Books, 2006)
A real mixed bag of information and activities, introducing everything from French language to cooking and customs.

BOOKS TO READ: FICTION

The Count of Monte Cristo (1845) and *The Three Musketeers* (1844) by Alexandre Dumas.
Both are rip-roaring adventure stories set back in the days of sword fighting and aristocratic treachery.

Le Grand Meaulnes Alain-Fournier (1913)
Set in the years before the First World War, this book has a very strong flavour of what life in rural France was like.

WEBSITES

http://uk.franceguide.com/
This is the official French Government tourist guide to France, and is packed with useful information about places to visit. Clicking on the 'Practical information' tab is a good place to start.

http://tinyurl.com/295hfm
This link will take you to the CIA (Central Intelligence Agency) web page about France. It's quite dry, but crammed full of useful information and statistics.

http://tinyurl.com/cm6mncs
This web page is a quick-reference guide to cycling facilities in French cities, and is part of a larger site called Rendezvous France, which is also useful.

Note to parents and teachers:
Every effort has been made by the Publishers to ensure that these websites are suitable for children, that they are of the highest educational value, and that they contain no inappropriate or offensive material. However, because of the nature of the Internet, it is impossible to guarantee that the contents of these sites will not be altered. We strongly advise that Internet access is supervised by a responsible adult.

INDEX